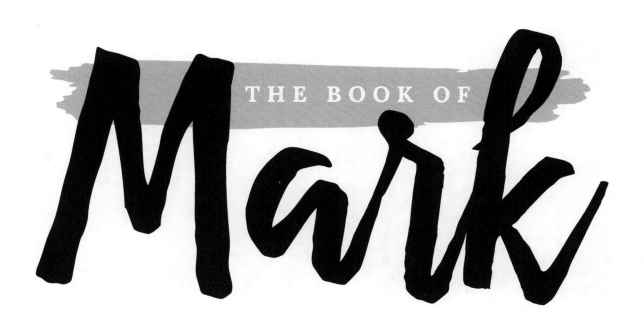

# THE BOOK OF
# Mark

## ONE CHAPTER A DAY

**GoodMorningGirls.org**

***Welcome to Good Morning Girls! We are so glad you are joining us.***

**G**od created us to walk with Him, to know Him, and to be loved by Him. He is our living well, and when we drink from the water He continually provides, His living water will change the entire course of our lives.

*Jesus said: "Whoever drinks of the water that I will give him will never be thirsty again. The water that I will give him will become in him a spring of water welling up to eternal life." ~ John 4:14 (ESV)*

So let's begin.

The method we use here at GMG is called the **SOAK** method.

- ❏ **S**—The S stands for *Scripture*—Read the chapter for the day. Then choose 1-2 verses and write them out word for word. (There is no right or wrong choice—just let the Holy Spirit guide you.)

- ❏ **O**—The O stands for *Observation*—Look at the verse or verses you wrote out. Write 1 or 2 observations. What stands out to you? What do you learn about the character of God from these verses? Is there a promise, command or teaching?

- ❏ **A**—The A stands for *Application*—Personalize the verses. What is God saying to you? How can you apply them to your life? Are there any changes you need to make or an action to take?

- ❏ **K**—The K stands for *Kneeling in Prayer*—Pause, kneel and pray. Confess any sin God has revealed to you today. Praise God for His word. Pray the passage over your own life or someone you love. Ask God to help you live out your applications.

SOAK God's word into your heart and squeeze every bit of nourishment you can out of each day's scripture reading. Soon you will find your life transformed by the renewing of your mind!

Walk with the King!

*Courtney*

*WomenLivingWell.org, GoodMorningGirls.org*

# Join the GMG Community

*Share your daily SOAK at 7:45am on **Facebook.com/GoodMorningGirlsWLW***

*Instagram: WomenLivingWell #GoodMorningGirls*

# GMG Bible Coloring Chart

| COLORS | KEYWORDS |
|---|---|
| PURPLE | God, Jesus, Holy Spirit, Saviour, Messiah |
| PINK | women of the Bible, family, marriage, parenting, friendship, relationships |
| RED | love, kindness, mercy, compassion, peace, grace |
| GREEN | faith, obedience, growth, fruit, salvation, fellowship, repentance |
| YELLOW | worship, prayer, praise, doctrine, angels, miracles,power of God, blessings |
| BLUE | wisdom, teaching, instruction, commands |
| ORANGE | prophecy, history, times, places, kings, genealogies, people, numbers, covenants, vows, visions, oaths, future |
| BROWN/GRAY | Satan, sin, death, hell, evil, idols, false teachers, hypocrisy, temptation |

# Introduction to the Book of Mark

I am so excited to begin our study in the book of Mark with you. We are going to be on the move with Christ! The book of Mark was written to the church in Rome, to prove beyond a shadow of a doubt, that Jesus Christ is the Messiah. Mark takes a different approach than the other gospels, focusing more on what Jesus did and less on what he said.

Mark starts with John the Baptist in the wilderness and moves quickly into the baptism of Jesus, the temptation in the desert, the calling of the disciples, the public ministry of Jesus Christ and then to the climax of Christ on the cross and the resurrection of our Savior.

Mark shows Jesus in a way that connects us intimately with Him. We see Him serving and eventually giving his life as the ultimate sacrifice, for our sins.

**Purpose:** To present the person and work of Jesus Christ.

**Author:** John Mark. Mark was not one of the original 12 disciples but was the accompaniment of Paul and Barnabas in the book of Acts. (If you struggle with second chances, this is a beautiful display of how the Lord can use us! John Mark struggled in the book of Acts and yet God still used him to pen a book that we still read today! To God be the glory!)

**Time Period:** Written between AD 55 and 65

Mark was probably the first gospel written and records more miracles than any of the others. All the other gospels combined, quote all but 31 verses of Mark.

**Key Verse:** "For even the Son of Man came not to be served but to serve, and to give his life as a ransom for many." Mark 10:45

**Major Themes of the Book of Mark:**

There are several major themes in the book of Acts that will not only teach us about the early church but are applicable to our own lives as believers.

1. **Jesus as the Son of God:** In the book of Mark, we see Jesus as God himself, come to earth. He is both fully God and fully man and his divinity is clearly seen in his power displayed through miracles.

2. **Jesus as a Servant:** Christ came to serve and the giving of His life was the ultimate act of service. With this example in mind, we also should serve God and others. Greatness in the kingdom of God comes through service.

3. **Jesus as a Miracle Worker:** Mark records more miracles than any other gospel and more miracles than sermons. Jesus didn't just tell people who He was, He showed them.

4. **The Spreading of the Gospel:** Jesus gave the gospel first to the Jews and then to the Gentiles as well. Jesus challenges his disciples' -and us- to go into all the world and preach the gospel. We need to reach out beyond our comfort zone and borders, to share the gospel everywhere!

The book of Mark is going to take us on a whirlwind trip back to the time of Christ. It is going to push us to live like Christ did. Be ready for action - and to take action! Be open to God moving in your life to serve others!

## Special Thanks

I want to extend a special thank you to Mandy Kelly, Rosilind Jukic, Bridget Childress and Misty Leask for your help with this journal. Your love, dedication and leadership to the Good Morning Girls ministry is such a blessing to all. Thank you for giving to the Lord.

~ Courtney

*And Jesus said to them,*

*"Follow me, and I will make you*

*fishers of men."*

*Mark 1:17*

## Reflection Question:

When Jesus called his first disciples, the Bible says they immediately dropped everything to follow him.

Have you ever felt God leading you in a new direction and how did you respond?

**S**—The S stands for *Scripture*

**O**—The O stands for *Observation*

**A**—The A stands for *Application*

**K**—The K stands for *Kneeling in Prayer*

*"Those who are well have no need of a physician,*

*but those who are sick.*

*I came not to call the righteous,*

*but sinners."*

*Mark 2:17*

**Reflection Question:**

Today we are reminded that Jesus ministered to those that others deemed unworthy.

Is there someone in your life who seems unworthy but who needs both the gospel and your love?

---

**S**—The S stands for *Scripture*

**O**—The O stands for *Observation*

**A**—The A stands for *Application*

**K**—The K stands for *Kneeling in Prayer*

*"For whoever does the will of God,*

*he is my brother and sister and mother."*

*Mark 3:35*

**Reflection Question:**

We are reminded as believers that we are all family.

How can this truth help fill a void in your life?  How have you already experienced this?

# Mark 3

**S**—The S stands for **Scripture**

**O**—The O stands for **Observation**

**A**—The A stands for **Application**

**K**—The K stands for **Kneeling in Prayer**

He said to them, "Why are you so afraid?

Have you still no faith?"

And they were filled with great fear

and said to one another,

"Who is this, that even the

wind and the sea obey him?"

Mark 4:40 & 41

**Reflection Question:**

Jesus has all authority over nature. Even the wind and waves obey Him.

How does knowing the power of Jesus, give you peace in the midst of your life storms?

**S**—The S stands for *Scripture*

**O**—The O stands for *Observation*

**A**—The A stands for *Application*

**K**—The K stands for *Kneeling in Prayer*

*"Do not fear, only believe."*

## Mark 5:36

**Reflection Question:**

Jesus reminds us that faith in him can heal us spiritually and even physically.

Name a time when faith in Jesus helped you overcome a struggle.

# Mark 5

**S**—The S stands for *Scripture*

**O**—The O stands for *Observation*

**A**—The A stands for *Application*

**K**—The K stands for *Kneeling in Prayer*

And he said to them,

"Come away by yourselves

to a desolate place

and rest a while."

Mark 6:31

**Reflection Question:**

When the apostles returned to Jesus from sharing the gospel, He told them to find a desolate place and rest awhile.

Where do you go to be alone, to seek God and replenish your soul?

# Mark 6

**S**—The S stands for *Scripture*

**O**—The O stands for *Observation*

**A**—The A stands for *Application*

**K**—The K stands for *Kneeling in Prayer*

These people honor me with their lips,

but their heart is far from me;

in vain do they worship me,

teaching as doctrines the commandments of men.

Mark 7:6,7

**Reflection Question:**

Today we are reminded to do things for the simple love of God and not because they are tradition.

Is there something that you have always done because you thought it was right, only to discover that is was a tradition and not God's law?

# Mark 7

**S**—The S stands for *Scripture*

**O**—The O stands for *Observation*

**A**—The A stands for *Application*

**K**—The K stands for *Kneeling in Prayer*

And calling the crowd to him with his disciples,

Jesus said,

"If anyone would come after me,

let him deny himself

and take up his cross and follow me."

Mark 8:34

**Reflection Question:**

We are commanded to take up our cross daily and follow Christ.

What does taking up your cross and denying yourself look like in your life?

# Mark 8

**S**—The S stands for *Scripture*

**O**—The O stands for *Observation*

**A**—The A stands for *Application*

**K**—The K stands for *Kneeling in Prayer*

*Jesus said,*

*"All things are possible*

*for the one who believes."*

*Mark 9:23*

**Reflection Question:**

Jesus said, all things are possible for the one that believes.

Do you believe the impossible for your life? How have you seen God work through your belief?

**S**—The S stands for *Scripture*

**O**—The O stands for *Observation*

**A**—The A stands for *Application*

**K**—The K stands for *Kneeling in Prayer*

*Many who are first will be last,*

*and the last first."*

Mark 10:31

**Reflection Question:**

Jesus tells us that we must be willing to leave behind everything for His sake.

What are you holding onto that is preventing you from following God in your life?

# Mark 10

**S**—The S stands for *Scripture*

**O**—The O stands for *Observation*

**A**—The A stands for *Application*

**K**—The K stands for *Kneeling in Prayer*

*"Whenever you stand praying, forgive,*

*if you have anything against anyone,*

*so that your Father also who is in heaven*

*may forgive you your trespasses."*

## Mark 11:25

**Reflection Question:**

Before we seek the Lord in prayer, we must forgive those that have wronged or hurt us.

Who do you need to offer forgiveness to today?

**S**—The S stands for *Scripture*

**O**—The O stands for *Observation*

**A**—The A stands for *Application*

**K**—The K stands for *Kneeling in Prayer*

And you shall love the Lord your God
with all your heart and with all your soul
and with all your mind and with all your strength.'
The second is this:
'You shall love your neighbor as yourself.'
There is no other commandment greater than these.

Mark 12:30,31

**Reflection Question:**

The greatest commandment is that we love God with all of our heart, soul, mind and strength and the second is that we love others as ourselves.

We don't always wake up in the morning ready to love God and others the way we should. How can we center our thoughts and minds on obeying these two greatest commandments every morning?

# Mark 12

**S**—The S stands for *Scripture*

**O**—The O stands for *Observation*

**A**—The A stands for *Application*

**K**—The K stands for *Kneeling in Prayer*

But concerning that day or that hour,

no one knows, not even the angels in heaven,

nor the Son, but only the Father.

Be on guard, keep awake.

For you do not know when the time will come.

Mark 13:32,33

**Reflection Question:**

We are called to watch for the coming of the Lord because we do not know the day or the hour of His return.

How are you watching for Jesus' return?

# Mark 13

**S**—The S stands for *Scripture*

**O**—The O stands for *Observation*

**A**—The A stands for *Application*

**K**—The K stands for *Kneeling in Prayer*

Watch and pray

that you may not enter into temptation.

The spirit is willing,

but the flesh is weak.

Mark 14:38

**Reflection Question:**

Often we have the best intentions to follow the Lord, as His disciples did, yet along the way we fail.

Is there something that is tempting you today? Watch yourself. Write a prayer telling God your temptations and ask him for strength to not fall.

# Mark 14

**S**—The S stands for *Scripture*

**O**—The O stands for *Observation*

**A**—The A stands for *Application*

**K**—The K stands for *Kneeling in Prayer*

*It was the third hour when they crucified him.*

*And the inscription of the charge against him read,*

*"The King of the Jews."*

*And with him they crucified two robbers,*

*one on his right and one on his left.*

*Mark 15:25~27*

**Reflection Question:**

Reflect on the pain and suffering Jesus endured for you.  He shed His blood for YOU!  All of our sins are forgiven because of His blood!  Sweet victory in Jesus!

Sing a song of worship today. Read a Psalm of praise. Write out a prayer of thanksgiving. Get on your knees, humble yourself before your King and give him glory and honor.

# Mark 15

**S**—The S stands for ***Scripture***

**O**—The O stands for ***Observation***

**A**—The A stands for ***Application***

**K**—The K stands for ***Kneeling in Prayer***

And he said to them,
"Go into all the world
and proclaim the gospel
to the whole creation.

Mark 16:15

**Reflection Question:**

We are called to go into the world and share the gospel with everyone.

How are you taking part in fulfilling the great commission?

# Mark 16

**S**—The S stands for *Scripture*

**O**—The O stands for *Observation*

**A**—The A stands for *Application*

**K**—The K stands for *Kneeling in Prayer*

Made in the USA
Coppell, TX
07 December 2023